Stripes and Stars

Sarah Fleming

Contents

OXFORD
UNIVERSITY PRESS

KV-063-052

Stars and stripes

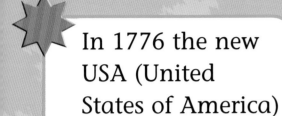

In 1776 the new USA (United States of America) had 13 states.

Alaska

CANADA

UNITED STATES OF AMERICA

In 1818 it had 20 states.

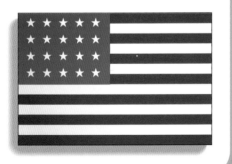

PACIFIC OCEAN

Hawaii

MEXICO

KEY

 The first 13 states, 1776
States joined by 1818
States joined by 1920
States joined by 1960

In 1920 it had 48 states.

How many stars are in each flag?

How many states has it got now? How can you tell?

The USA flag, today

ATLANTIC OCEAN

Zebras

Fit the last bits into the jigsaw.

A

B

C

D

E

F

G

H

How many zebras can you see?

Can you see eight differences between the photos?

How many zebras are drinking?

Star cat

Can you see this cat in the stars?

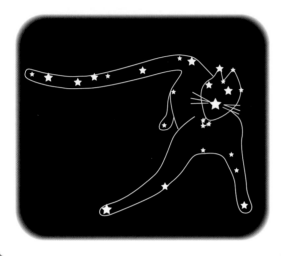

Can you see this shape?

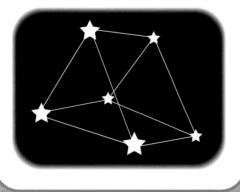

Can you see this snake?

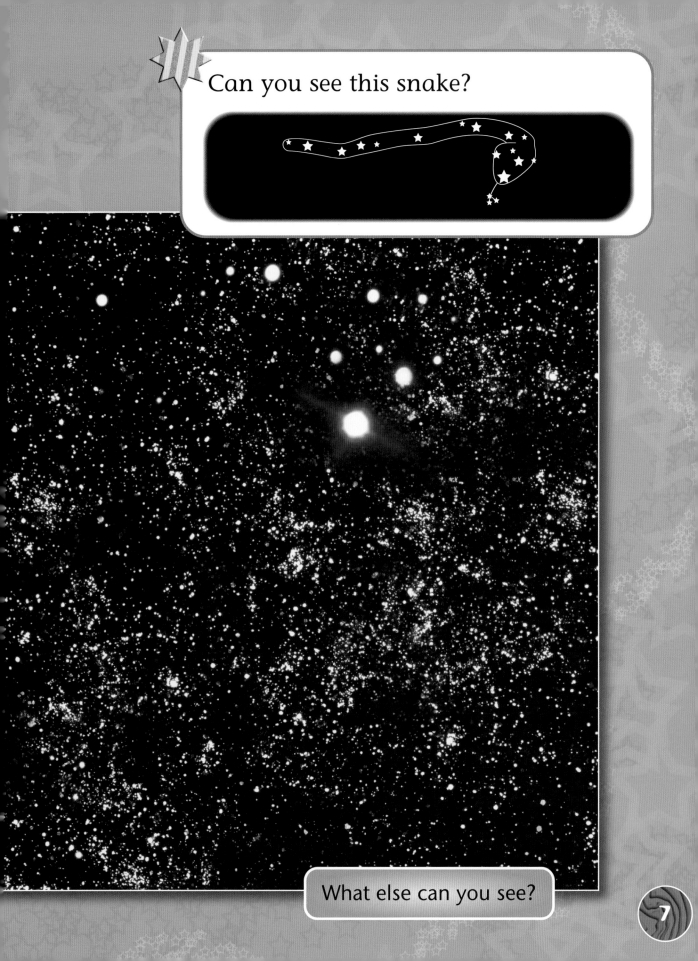

What else can you see?

Flags

How many flags have:
- stars with six points?
- yellow stars?
- only one star?

Morocco

Tunisia

North
America

South
America

Cuba

Venezuela

Brazil

Chile

Ghana

Cameroon

Angola

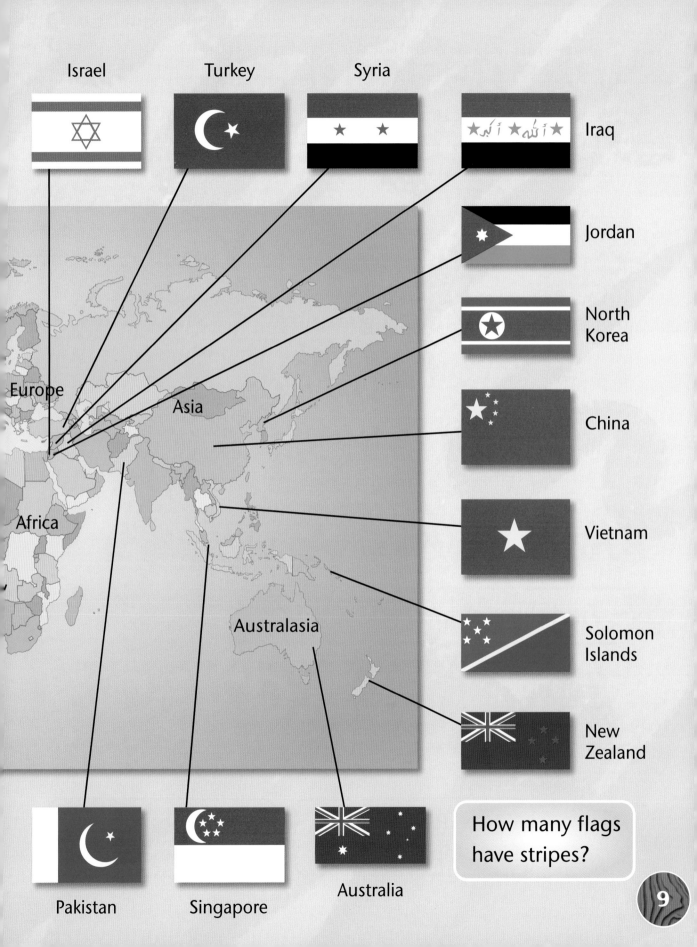

Israel

Turkey

Syria

Iraq

Jordan

North Korea

China

Vietnam

Solomon Islands

New Zealand

Europe

Asia

Africa

Australasia

Pakistan

Singapore

Australia

How many flags have stripes?

9

Do cheetahs have stripes?

 Find these stripes.

Where does a cheetah have stripes?

Where does a gazelle have stripes?

Fishy!

A

B

C

D

Which fish is which?

Which fish has this fin?

Starfish

How many:
- starfish?
- shells?
- crabs?
- jaws?

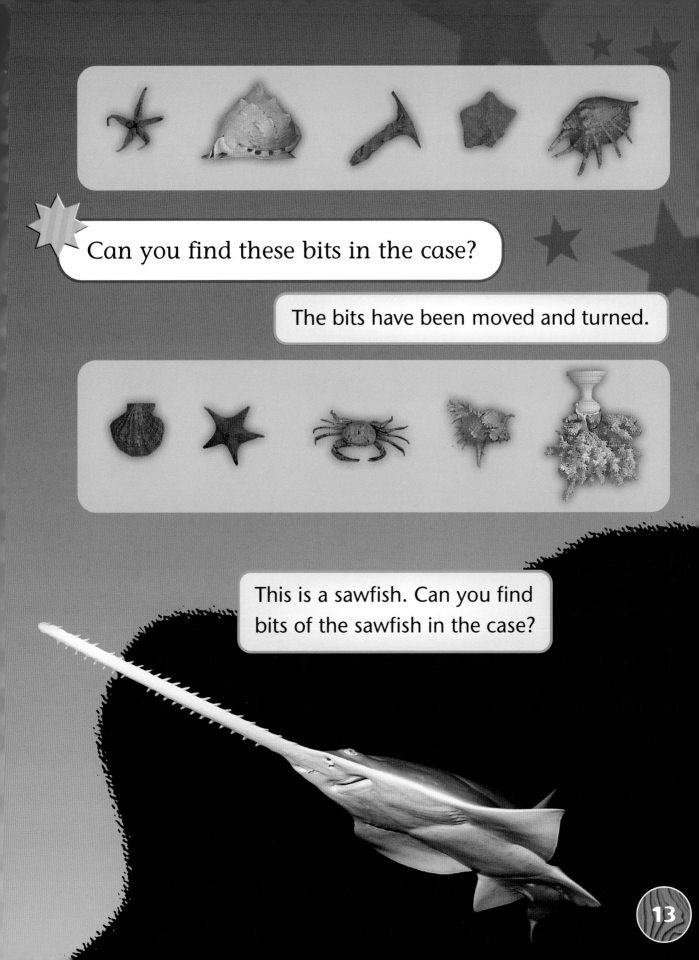

Can you find these bits in the case?

The bits have been moved and turned.

This is a sawfish. Can you find bits of the sawfish in the case?

Ball game

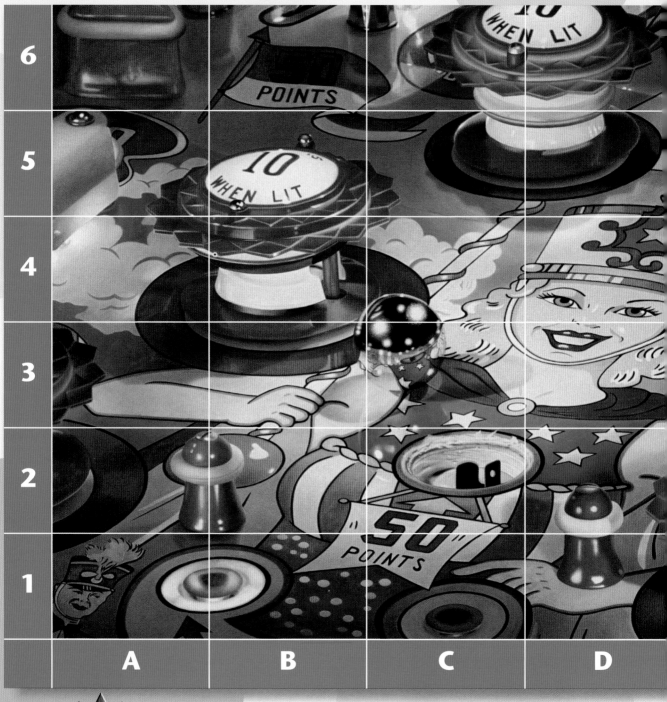

	A	B	C	D
6				
5				
4				
3				
2				
1				

14

This is box number D4.
Why is it called D4?

E	F

Give box numbers for:
- the box with most stars
- four boxes with the number ten

What is in box:
- B3?
- D3?
- F2?

How many stars can you see?

Starry night

 How many:
- stars?
- stripes?

What are the stripes made of?